T0149537

NO ONE KNOWS BUT ME

NO ONE KNOWS BUT ME

AND OTHER POEMS

Briana L. Boggio

NO ONE KNOWS BUT ME
AND OTHER POEMS

iUniverse books may be ordered through booksellers or by contacting:

iUniverse
1663 Liberty Drive
Bloomington, IN 47403
www.iuniverse.com
1-800-Authors (1-800-288-4677)

ISBN: 978-1-5320-5664-2 (sc)
ISBN: 978-1-5320-5665-9 (e)

Library of Congress Control Number: 2018910715

Print information available on the last page.

iUniverse rev. date: 09/07/2018

Special Thanks

I would like to thank my friends
and family for their support,
and all those people who
made these poems possible.

THROUGHOUT THE YEAR

Graduation

I can't wait to leave this place.
I will forever remember your face.
I thought I would die,
but now I think I'll cry.
I will miss every one of you.
I hope that you do too.
My heart will break and crack.
I hope we all come back
to see your smiling faces.
You will always be in my heart.
You are a very special part
of a very hectic life.
I love every one of you.
I hope you know this is true.
I will always remember it here.
I liked the high school years.
Then I ask each of you why,
why must it be goodbye?
Goodbye is not forever,
but forgetting you would be never.

Spring

Seeing everything sparkle
from the dew left behind,
hearing birds chirp
as it relaxes my mind,
feeling the cool breeze
as it carries scents of spring,
while everything awakens,
it all seems inspiring.
The animals frolic
in the beautiful green,
the flowing river
looking so serene.
With nothing disturbed
I quietly slip away.
With a glimmer in my eye
I enjoy the beautiful day.

Days of Summer

Beautiful colors of green everywhere,
the smell of freshly cut grass in the air,
sunshine warming everything,
hearing the happy birds sing,
enjoying water sports with friends,
always out and about till the summer ends,
mowing the yard as your day begins,
you feel the sun on your skin,
appreciating every wonderful day while it's here,
knowing that the winter will soon appear,
breathing in the great smells of the air,
going on through the days without care,
reading a book or just sitting in the sun
as we relish it and have fun.

The Day Just for You

Glad that you are my dad—
there is no better to be had.
Making you proud of what I do—
a fact you know to be true.
Happy when I get to see your face—
there is nothing that could replace
getting to hear from you when you call.
You are the best dad of all.
No one, not even I, could ask for more.
Just being your child is what I live for.

Vampire

Awake with a strong desire
that burns as hot as fire,
you are agile and cunning,
altogether stunning,
moving as quiet as a whisper,
making the air around me stir,
sending chills down my spine
and fear through my bloodline
and yet I am still drawn
like an innocent pawn.
Though I am your prey,
I wish you to stay.
Like a moth to a flame
you are drawn just the same,
not knowing what binds us—
love or that you're ravenous—
following you into the dark
as you leave your mark.

October 31

The holiday that brings out the weird
and even the things most feared,
known as the bridge to the world of the dead.
Be sure to lock your doors before bed.
Spirits and witches roaming around,
ghosts revisiting us from underground,
it was a day known as All Hallows' Eve.
In today's world most people disbelieve.
You get candy, games, and toys,
things that most everyone enjoys.
From time to time it is true
that you could happen upon a shrew,
past dangers no one knows,
still being startled when the wind blows.

The Hunt

Waiting in the early hours of the morning,
sitting quietly and patiently for a stirring,
then finally something shows itself.
Its antlers are just the right size of perfect.
You set up your sites just right.
Then you take in a slow, steadying breath
and slowly let it out as you pull the trigger.
Your hunted then falls to the ground.
Feeling victorious you go claim your kill,
taking it home to skin it and butcher it,
excited to do it again next year.

Frost

Seeing it sparkle and shine,
creating its own striking design,
making the air fresh and clean,
covering everything in a sheen,
transforming everything into a diamond,
this type of weather I am most fond,
watching all things glisten,
dancing in the rays of the sun,
with a crisp chill in the air.

What Below Zero?

That horrible chill that's in the air,
making it cold no matter what you wear,
layers upon layers, but it's still no use,
feeling like it's some kind of abuse—
you long to be indoors with the heat,
knowing again the cold you'll meet.
Once you do, the cold air stings your face.
All the memories of warmth erase
longing to be in a nice warm bed,
having the end of day just ahead,
finally being nice and warm indoors,
no more of this nonsense outdoors.

Pure Snowflakes

Soft and white fluffs,
little pillowy clouds,
falling slowly from above,
gently kissing my cheeks—
they calm the night,
covering everything in sparkles,
making the air new.

The Hate of Winter

Here it comes every year.
I hate the days that it draws near,
knowing it will be cold and icy
and all driving will be dicey,
not wanting to leave my bed,
hearing the alarm in my head,
with my house not getting warm,
not looking forward to the next storm,
sick of the frost and the cold,
for this weather I am too old.

Winter

All the beautiful blues and whites—
to be so lucky to behold such sights.
Smelling the crisp and clean air
brings me everything except despair.
Wanting to build a snowman
just for the simple fact that I can,
coming inside for a nice warm drink
while I sit there content and think
about the wonderful scene out the window,
seeing all the clean white snow,
watching the flakes fall in our downtime—
this is why we love the wintertime.

Right Around the Corner

Seeing the sun come out to play,
warming even a cold day,
melting the snow and ice,
it makes everything look nice.
Getting closer to the warmer days,
sitting, tanning in the sun's rays,
I cannot wait for that time
when the temperatures start to climb.
I embrace the cold that's almost over
and wait for the season to cross over.
Spring is so close and so near,
I can't believe it's practically here.

PATRIOTIC SIDE

September 11

What happened on September 11th?
Some of you think buildings fell down;
others see painful losses, family, loved ones.
Many people were lost that day.
So many people made it through.
Thousands of people were hurt by this.
Some people say, "Oh well, move on."
How can you move on when this happens?
What do you do when their birthday comes?
Do you just forget about it and move on?
How can they pick up and move on?
What happened was a tragedy,
not an accident or mistake.
This was murder, an act of war.
Now we are all to stand together,
for we are the United States,
and united we shall stand.

The Troops

With brothers and sisters standing by my side,
knowing that they are there gives me pride.
I feel strong and able with our mission at hand
as we fight vigorously and victoriously for our land.
We serve each and every one of you proudly
as we feel you cheering for us loudly.
Every morning it's on with our combat boots
while you back home put on fresh clean suits.
We walk and walk, not seeing end in sight
while you get to tuck your kids in at night.
Very tired, in pain, and wanting so much sleep,
constantly moving because of a promise to keep,
we will be fine as long as we don't have a snag
that would cause us to come home under the American flag.

Old Glory

The American flag has meanings all throughout it.
There is no part of the flag that is meaningless in the least bit.
The thirteen colonies are represented by the red and the white.
Red is meant to show the blood sacrificed in the fight.
White has the meaning of courage and bravery; freedom is blue,
fifty stars that symbolize the fifty states, as you all knew.
Seeing it in its beautiful form, flying in the wind, is stimulating.
Appreciating the flag for its meanings that are motivating—
it is so peaceful and majestic when there is a slight breeze.
Seeing the colors as they just wave slowly, looking at ease—
when I see it flying true it touches me to my soul,
like nothing else ever could as a whole.

The Pledge

People say that we pledge to a piece of cloth.
It is not the cloth we pledge but the symbol,
symbol of loyalty and support for our country.
That's why I pledge allegiance to the flag.

Others think it is throwing religion on us,
the "under God" is meaning any God,
and the pledge was meant to teach patriotism,
so I pledge allegiance to the flag.

Pledging the flag with everyone standing together—
that is showing unity in our country.
Unity is something we all want and need,
so why not pledge allegiance to the flag?

Life in POL

Big, green, and bulky—
that's what they give me.
The big, long fuel truck—
my favorite is Chuck.
That would be truck Charlie.
My job makes me happy.
Getting to fuel the C-130s—
it's as easy as a breeze.
Getting to drive this big thing,
for me it is just amazing.
Issuing jet fuel like it's no one's business
has me doing good with fitness,
dragging the hose to the plane,
such an opportunity that's insane.

CDCs

I sit down and start to read,
hoping nothing will intercede.
I focus and answer the questions
that they have at all the sections.
I start losing my motivation
and start gaining confusion,
trying hard to stay awake,
wishing I could just take a break,
studying day in and day out,
feeling the knowledge fade out,
thinking this would be a breeze,
studying my warehouse CDCs.

Army

Getting up at the break of day,
always doing what they say,
working so hard just to keep going,
never having a chance at slowing—
how I miss those army days.

We march with cadence sounding,
with all our hearts pounding,
hearing the jingle of our dog tags,
running with our fifty-pound bags—
I miss those army days.

Doing push-ups until you can't move,
continually till we all improve,
pushing yourself on the obstacle course,
knowing if you fail there's no remorse—
oh, how I miss those army days.

SPLENDOR OF NATURE

Beaches

The beautiful golden sands
that run through your hands,
the cool blue flowing over your feet
feels amazing in this horrible heat.
Waves that break and crack
against the rocks they smack,
knowing to many it is a home,
yes, even in the foam
the beach is a wondrous place,
so big and full of space,
feeling the sand under your toes
or the water when the wind blows,
many peaceful sounds in the air,
having the breeze in your hair,
making everything serene,
unlike anything you've ever seen.

Mermaids

They swim every which way,
always hard to see what you saw,
thinking your mind's at play.
Their beautiful tails of many colors,
they have bodies of a lady.
You look again, but they are gone.
Blaming it on the day being shady,
they swim fast and sleek,
jumping feet out of the water.
Taking your mind by surprise,
they play around like a sea otter.
Wanting to see her again,
wondering if what you saw was true,
knowing people will think you're crazy,
you continue searching the deep blue.

Sparks

As they spark with a loud boom,
making everyone look from the room,
they are bright green and reds,
with blues and yellows to turn heads.
Fireworks are always a glamorous sight,
the way they light up the night.
There are some that zig and zag
and some that look like the flag,
having a couple that start on the ground
that end up flying around,
some that can go into water—
that is usually when it gets hotter,
seeing the fireworks flying in the sky,
following where they go before they die.

The Dancing Light

Flickering this way and that,
always dancing on the walls,
    like that of a scared bat
when trapped in the light—
    the movement is soothing
as it glows ever so bright.
The lights I then turn out
    so I may join the dance
before it starts to burn out.

Gentle Giants

These creatures are big, beautiful, and gentle.
The largest was said to be thirteen feet tall.
Elephant babies are the cutest thing.
Their feet and trunks are used for listening.
They are highly sensitive and caring creatures,
with their trunks as their defining feature.
They can't jump, but they walk without a sound,
with their special padded feet hitting the ground.
Their ears circulate blood, cooling them when it's hotter,
swimming and using their nose as a snorkel in water.

Clear Skies

They sky is black as night,
with lightning flashing so bright,
the thunder booming so loud
you can't hear the crowd.
Rain starts streaming.
I watch while dreaming.
Thunder, like a beating drum,
makes me start to hum.
Lightning that lights up the earth,
showing everything it's worth,
the air smells so fresh and clean,
making such a surreal scene.

The Beauty of the Night

Stars glistening in the night,
the moon shining so bright,
the air clean and uplifting—
you can feel the night air shifting.
No sounds to be heard,
not even the chirp of a bird,
no owls hooting in the dark,
nor a dog letting out a bark,
just as calm as can be,
not seeing anything beastly,
seeing the stars in the big sky,
I go inside, telling the night goodbye.

The Dance of Fire

See how fire sparkles in the night.
It puts off heat with its brilliant light.
It snaps and cracks and pops
and heats the faces of the rocks,
throwing embers into the sky
while you follow with your eye.
The fire is so peaceful and serene,
it makes everything look so clean.
Watching the flames and their dance,
it makes you feel as you're in a trance.
Contained in its stone band,
it is unlikely to get out of hand.
Seeing a campfire puts me at rest.
Beauty of a night fire is the best.

La Luna

Looking up at the moon and its glory
as it shines down, making the earth glow,
wanting to see it from an observatory,
to get to see every dead volcano and crater—
the moon is an amazing thing to see.
With all the wonders of the world,
getting to see the moon would be greater.

The Moon

It's so bright and alluring
as it keeps my gaze,
calming my heart and soul,
stopping tears in their tracks,
so bright in the darkness,
leaving me feeling safe.
I watch as my worries melt.
It helps me take a deep breath.
Seeing the moon in the clouds
becomes hypnotizing and soothing,
forgetting all the sad thoughts
until I lose its glowing sight,
causing it all to come back.
Tears start filling my eyes.
My heart starts beating erratically
until the night I see it again.

The Eyes of the Heavens

The beautiful stars that glitter in the night sky,
seeing them flicker before my eye
as I find the amazing constellations
that open us to our imaginations—
just thinking of how hard they would be to draw,
I smile when I find constellation Norma.
Some of the stars glow brightly,
while others seem to dim ever so slightly.
It's so wonderful when there isn't a cloud in sight,
nothing in the way to put out the light,
sitting there just looking above,
with so many things to think of,
wanting to explore all the stars out there,
just floating around in the open air.

Butterflies

Beautiful they are when flying around,
not making the slightest sound,
all their colors showing in the sunshine,
seeing them start to intertwine.
They are so unique in their colorful designs,
colors separated by intricate lines.
They are as delicate as a snowflake.
Touching their wings would be a mistake.
You barely feel them when they land,
holding them gently in your hand.
Seeing the majesty of butterflies,
you will not believe your eyes.

Nature's Beauty

Their bodies are tall and sleek.
Some think they are a freak.
So beautiful with a camel-like form,
they only live where it's warm
and are the tallest living creature.
The neck is their greatest feature.
They sleep only twenty minutes a day,
at which they can stand or lay.
Their tongues are a gray or dark blue
that doesn't get sunburned as they chew.
After being born they drop six feet to earth,
learning to run ten hours after birth.

Killer Whales

Possibly as many as sixteen different classes,
sometimes they hunt in the masses.
They are said to be very large dolphins.
Some of their prey include penguins
measuring lengths up to thirty-three feet.
Seals, sea lions, and other marine mammals they eat.
Some killer whales reach one hundred years old.
That is something amazing to behold—
watching them swim, looking so glorious
as they approach everything so curious.

Out in Space

Space is so vast and so deep,
not hearing even a slightest peep,
but seeing stars that die away
is much more than we can say.
The atmosphere is filled with open space.
There is much more to embrace,
with so many galaxies billions of light-years away,
not knowing the end of a day,
making the world seem really small,
asking what's out there after all.

Messengers from Above

They fly everywhere, having no care,
carrying with them such flair,
looking at their complete allure,
you can only be sure.

You see them flying above you
against the deep dark blue.
Their wings are filled with every tone.
They never fly alone.

Their wings span more than arm's length,
so graceful with amazing strength.
They came from heaven above
from a place some haven't heard of.

Angels

Angels soaring up above,
angels soaring down below,
angels all among us,
so why do so many go?

They are here to protect.
They are here to love.
As I look around,
I see them like a dove.

With their wings spread out
as beautiful as I'd ever see,
glowing, radiant, and captivating,
filling us with glee.

Yet some still pass,
wanting to meet the grave.
No matter how difficult,
the angels can't save.

THE GREAT WHITE
AND MORE

Deep Blue Sea

They are very strong and fierce.
Through your skin their teeth will pierce.
They swim with incredible speed,
looking for something on which to feed.
They can hear distances up to eight hundred feet—
that seems frighteningly neat.
Sharks can be very big or very small;
no matter the size, they still have a downfall.
A lightweight skeletal structure
mostly of cartilage is their substructure.
Their eyesight is very keen,
bitten before you ever knew you were seen.

Mysteries

Gliding monsters of the deep,
along the floor they creep,
with white eyes as black as night
only until they bite.

You fight and fight for air,
knowing that no one is there.
You groan with such pain.
Slowly you start to wane.

It swims with great poise,
making no more noise.
It continues to move on,
and then it is gone.

Proceeding to drift,
looking so cunning and swift,
it looks for its next meal,
taking the life of a seal.

The Hammerhead

Did you know there are nine diverse
species of the hammerhead shark?
Knowing that almost makes it worse.
They like to feed on stingrays,
using their heads to pin rays to the seafloor.
They eat smaller fish and octopuses,
attacked before they knew they were done for.
Often being hunted just for their fins,
they get tossed back into the sea.
Without fins to support them, they tend to drown.
They can find prey in water even if it's murky.
Living between twenty and thirty years of age,
they can be the size of an average car.
Being any color of green or grey brown,
they are more amazing than a blazing star.

Gliding Monsters

Gliding along day after day,
some traveling a long way
in search of their next meal—
anything that strikes an appeal.
Some gentle, while some alarming,
some even strike you as charming,
most of which are vulnerable
to poaching that's intolerable.
Their fins are used for soup,
then the body is tossed into a group,
just left for dead and misspent—
this happens all too frequent.
While some people go on not knowing
the threat of sharks is growing.

Sharp Teeth

They bite and tear and rip,
not loosening their grip.
Shaking their head side to side,
you start to feel your body divide.
They stab and chew and grind,
not leaving any evidence behind.
Bull sharks have 478 pounds of force.
Their teeth are rugged and course.
Shark teeth are found for creativeness.
Most items made are for decorativeness,
ranging from all different sizes,
the bigger ones seen as prizes.

When a Shark Bites

You are swimming, minding your own,
when you hear the crunching of bone.
Realizing that something's bitten into you,
stranded and alone, not knowing what to do,
the shark pulls you under while you shout,
questioning if your lungs will give out.
The shark then lets go of your limb.
Racing to the surface, you awkwardly swim.
Your head breaks surface as you gasp for air,
hoping that someone, anyone, is there.
All you see is land forty-seven meters away.
Swimming, you hope not to be prey
as you finally drag yourself onshore,
swearing not to swim in the ocean anymore.

Pale Catshark

Why are they so feared and despised?
They always seem to be getting criticized.
Sharks are not vicious creatures.
True that some of them have terrifying features;
however, others are small and gentle.
If they bite you it's mostly accidental.
The cutest little one is the pale catshark.
It is known to live down in the dark.
It is, at most, 8.27 inches small,
but the great white is my favorite most of all.

FEELINGS FROM THE INSIDE

Life Is Hard

Life is hard when you're alone.
When no one is there to help you,
no one is there to hold you.

People don't understand.
They push you away
when you need them most.

Life is hard, so get your friend.
Sit for hours, and talk.
Just be with someone
when life is hard.

Love

Love is your touch,
the look in your eyes,
the way you care,
how I feel when
we are together.

When we are apart,
it only gets stronger.
Love is more
than just skin deep;
it goes to the core.

Love is a feeling,
a feeling that won't die.
Love is the way I feel,
feel about you.
This we have is love.

No One Knows But Me

My heart loves only one.
My eyes see only two.
My mind knows only three.
My heart aches all day long.
The tears flow throughout the day.
No one knows but me.

The pain gets stronger.
I keep it all to myself.
My head's filled with confusion.
There are so many hearts on the line.
Everyone goes on with their day,
because no one knows but me.

I toss and turn in the night.
There's only one I can't let go.
There's one that doesn't even know.
I sit at home alone,
wondering constantly what to do,
and no one knows but me.

The Love in My Heart

My heart feels for one person,
but that person isn't even here.
No one knows of the love I carry
or how much joy it brings me
just to hear your voice in my ear.
I lie awake, wondering if you're alone.
My heart grows wings when you call.

My heart belongs to no one else.
It became numb to the world when you left.
You're the only one who makes it dance.
I have told you how I felt,
and I've always felt the same.
I've tried to move on, but it makes no sense,
although you are so very far away.

You still bring me happiness as friends,
but my heart will never let you go.
I keep everyone out now.
You are the only one who I let in,
and I love you without knowing it.
You are always there in my heart
and always on my mind.

Could It Be Love?

Your eyes brighten my day.
Your smile brightens my world.
Your touch warms my heart.
You make me feel important.

I like being able to hold you.
I feel comfort being with you.
I like seeing you when I wake,
seeing you looking back at me.

I smile when I think of you.
My heart flutters when I see you.
I get chills when you kiss me.
My heart beats rapidly for you.

Downhearted

Tears roll down my face.
I'm surrounded by empty space.
My heart aches all day.
My mind goes every which way.
My entire body is weak.
I have problems trying to speak.
I keep it all bottled inside.
My pain I choose to hide.
I'm hurting inside, so much pain,
like I'm being pulled by a rein.
I lie awake, pondering.
My brain continues wandering.
I long to be truly joyful
instead of being sorrowful.
When people look, I smile.
It'll be there only for a while.
They can't see the pain I hide.
They don't know I'm dying inside.
I'm in a dark place.
I long to see your face.
You took my smile away,
but I want you to stay.
I love you so much.
I need to feel your touch.
The pain I ignore.
I don't want to hurt anymore.

True Feelings

So I thought my life was done.
I thought I found my one
until the night I saw you.
My heart is no longer blue.
I didn't love him with all my heart.
That I know now that we're apart.

My face glows when I see you,
and he doesn't have a clue.
You make my life complete.
I'm glad Chris had us meet.
I'm the happiest I've ever been.
To be without you would be a sin.

I want to make you the happiest man.
I'll do the best that I can.
You are the one of my dreams.
Our love won't rip at the seams.
Our love I can say is real,
something that no one could ever steal.

Letting Go

It is hard to do
when you love someone,
but sometimes you have to
in order to move on.

I am trying my best
to pick up the pieces.
I have been put to the test,
and I will succeed.

My heart's in pain,
but I keep driving on.
Even though it's insane,
I will come out on top.

It hurts to be alone
when you want happiness.
I will take what I've been shown,
and I will be strong.

My Angel

When you touch me I feel complete.
When you kiss me I melt.
When you hold me I crumble in your arms.
My dreams are only about you.
Every time I hear your voice,
my problems disappear.
You make me so happy
that when I see you I can't stop smiling.
You brighten even the darkest day.
To see your beautiful smile breaks my heart.
Your laugh is so heavenly.
You must be an angel.

Shattered

My world comes crashing down,
so I wear a frown.
My heart now shatters,
acting like nothing matters.
Two are to blame.
We've been put to shame.
I think about you and me
back when we were happy.

Broken

If it's true that everyone has someone created for them,
then I am doomed to be alone forever.
You were my life, my heart, my soul.
You completed me. My love for you was strong.
You were my light, my dark, my happy, my sad,
but no matter what, you were always mine—
my lover, my friend, my half. Now you're hers.

Letting My Guard Down

Feeling my heart race
when I see his handsome face,
I start feeling happy again,
with no more worries of pain.
Holding each other feels right,
making my heart take flight.
I smile when I hear from you,
knowing that you do too.
Then something goes askew,
and you tell me adieu.
As soon as you avert,
I begin feeling hurt.
Tears start flowing,
wondering why I let you in,
with my soul in ruin.
Now I need to be strong once more
so that I won't hit the floor.
I keep everyone away,
with hopes that someday
we can start anew,
but that is up to you.

Not Knowing

What are these experiences?
I need to come to my senses.
Not sure of what I feel.
It all seems so surreal.
It was too soon to be love—
that is just unheard of.
But there was something there,
'cause inside it started a flair.
I don't want to say farewell.
That would send me through hell.
So for now I'll close my eyes
and wait for the sun to rise.

At Peace

Dark but still so bright
with stars glowing like light,
everything so tranquil,
it leaves my body still,
sending quivers up my spine
as I gaze at the skyline.
The beauty takes my breath away,
and there I stay,
admiring such an astonishment.
I found myself content
with everything at peace.
I can finally release
the troubles of the day
and slowly drift away,
so my mind may repose
in a place that no one knows.

With You

To see the sun in your eyes,
to hear beauty in your voice,
listening to your laugh
is what I get when I'm with you.

Seeing how gentle you are,
knowing how much you care,
to feel your lips on my neck
is what I get when I'm with you.

Excited to see your face,
overjoyed just to hug you,
wanting to hold you close
is what I get when I'm with you.

Impossible

When you love someone
the way that I love you,
then letting go for me
is the most impossible thing,
like cutting wire with scissors,
chopping a tree with a rock,
or walking on water.
There's no healing without you,
just getting used to the pain.
There is a rift in my heart
that can only be filled
with your family and your love.
I'm deadened to things around me.
Only your Power can fix me.
You let go so abruptly,
taking away my everything.
I find it hard to breathe
when people say your name.
When I close my eyes
all I see is your face.
Our love is wound so deep.
Losing you hurts in my bones.
I love you more than I love me.

Always There

You are always there for me.
When my heart gets broken you hold me.
When I get home you greet me,
next to me every time I drink.
In the nights I cry myself to sleep.
There the nights I don't sleep
and with me everywhere I travel,
so this goes out to you,
never being alone,
because loneliness is always there.

Healing

Things to do that I should have done,
I should have known you weren't the one,
picking me up just to tear me back down,
seeing now how I'll always be treated.
No matter how much I hope, it's always repeated.
This time around I must let you go.
Even if it pains me I must be free to grow.
There's someone out there to love me,
so from now on I'll just let you be.

Undone Betrayal, or Enlightened

Being deceived is painful,
but by a friend it's worse.
To think you actually cared
as you stand there averse.
I went to you for everything.
How could I be so blind,
thinking you were different?
I thought you were true and kind.
You were always so sweet.
Knowing now it was a front—
you could have been honest
even if you were blunt.

Being Torn

I am struggling with two,
being pulled this way and that,
not knowing what to do.
I can't focus on anything.
I find myself thinking about
one in particular,
putting myself in doubt
of how I truly feel.
I don't want to get wounded.
In that, I know what to do,
but I can't seem to clear my head,
knowing all along that it's wrong,
but I continue untruly,
burdening myself with guilt,
and no one knows but me.

New Love

Smiling when I see your face,
I walk into your embrace,
never wanting your arms to leave,
feeling like it's all make-believe,
wanting all day just to hold you,
for it to be just us two.
Getting to lie next to you at night
I find to be such a delight,
enjoying every minute with you,
no matter what we do.
The way you make me blush
has me telling you to hush.

FAMILY AND FRIENDS

Friends

Is a friend someone
who cries with you
and laughs with you,
someone to be there
when you need them,

to hold you when
you lose someone
or to help you out
when you're hurt
or having problems?

They are someone you trust,
tell your most deepest secrets,
someone who loves you
because you are all of
these and many more.

My Best Friend

A lot of secrets make a bond.
A strong bond makes a pact.
A solid pact makes a great friendship.
That friendship becomes very powerful,
and that belongs only to you.

Twin Birthday

Happy birthday to me. Happy birthday to you.
Every year I wonder what we will do.
Together we're one more year older.
Age, as they say, is in the eye of the beholder.

For so many years it's been the two of us.
Here and there we would make a fuss,
but today we celebrate together our birthday.
To most people it is just another day.

It is more than that to me.
It is a day when I am truly happy
sharing this celebratory day with you.
I say happy birthday to me and to you.

Mother

My mother is my best friend.
She is a shoulder when I need
and gives me hugs when I'm sad.
She guides me through life
and keeps me driving on.

Mom is my number one lady.
She's behind me 100 percent.
She is there no matter what.
With her as my mom,
I don't need to wish for anything.

The Twins

I have a twin who's older than me—
not by much, just forty-six minutes, you see.
He was taller first for 6,205 days.
His hair is light brown like mine,
but his is growing a thin line.
He works hard in his yard when he has time.
I work on poems—that's no crime.
He likes to hunt and fish with Dad.
Seeing them do things makes me glad.
I like to shoot guns like my twin,
but when I shoot better than him I grin.
He is my twin every day, no matter how.
There's just no getting rid of him now.

Dedicated to Brent Boggio

The Redhead

She's awesome, and she's true.
She will always be there for you.
She tells it like it is,
with her being such a wiz,
and they call her the redhead.

She'll always be there when you call
and willing to help you when you fall.
She will never tell you she told you so,
because she knows deep down you know,
and they call her the redhead.

She's always there to have your back,
even when you're deserving a smack.
She will help you with anything you need,
as long as her words you heed,
and they call her the redhead.

Her family and mountain she loves the most.
She missed them terribly when she was on the coast.
So many things fill her heart.
We will miss her when she is apart,
and we call her the redhead.

Dedicated to Dawn Charron

Cousin

My dearest, you are always there
when I need you, as much as air.
You always know how to cheer me up.
My tears never overflow from your cup.
We are the best of friends.
We last longer than most trends.
You are my dearest cugina.
Together we laugh like a hyena.

Dedicated to Chantel Nelson

Cinq-Mars

Lieutenant Colonel Cinq-Mars, Commander of LRS—
she was that and so much more to us,
always helping those in need,
assisting those troubled to proceed.
In spare time she was a soccer coach.
No matter what, she was easy to approach.
She's part of the "big sister, big brother."
She was like the LRS den mother.
When we needed it
she went to bat for anyone and never quit.
She will always be the best we've had.
I'm proud to say she is our comrade.
Dedicated to Lieutenant Colonel Jen Cinq-Mars

TREASURES THAT I LOST

Grandpa

Grandpa is a special word,
a word for someone like you.
You were patient and kind.
You made everyone laugh.
You were always full of jokes.
There was no anger with you in the room.
You taught us grandkids everything:
how to drive, to stay young,
and how to make it count.
You were strict when we needed it.
You were gentle when we were sad,
and now you are gone.
But I can still hear your jokes,
hear your laugh, see your smile.
I know that you're with us,
helping us through everything,
because you're our grandpa.

Dedicated to Jim Boggio

Georgia Wieber Kline

Georgia, mom, sister, aunt, grandma—
all these words for one terrific lady.
She was always the one who
made us smile. When family and
friends came together, it was
always around her.
Her heart always took us in,
just like her house. Both were big
and had room for all of us and
then some. Whether in need or just
to say hello, she always greeted
everyone with open arms and a
smile. Now she greets us
every morning when we wake up.
She is always in our hearts and
our souls. She is with us all day
every day until we get the
chance to see her again. I know
that when we do it will be
as though she was on a long vacation—
a glorious and happy moment,
as if she never left us.

Dedicated to Georgia Kline

Robert Armstrong

I know our time was brief.
Even still it causes me grief.
When I see pictures of you
it hurts all the way through.
I recall the sight of your smile.
Glad I knew you for a while.
Remember the sound when you snicker,
seeing the light in your eye flicker.
I never said I forgave you.
I want you to know it's true.
You were such a bright person.
You were never one to be withdrawn.
I'd always thought someday,
not knowing that would go away,
seeing now you were in pain,
having to go through strain,
everyone is in such sorrow,
knowing we won't see you tomorrow.

Dedicated to Robert Armstrong

A Treasured Soul

It's always hard to lose someone.
I'm hurt losing someone I barely knew.
Looking around I see the effects on everyone—
on all the friends who lost him,
on the parents losing their only son,
on the sister losing her only brother,
even on the dog that lost his dad.
Robert was loved by all who knew him.
He was always fun to be around.
Knowing now that the family is incomplete,
the gatherings lost the life of the party.
There's always going to be that space for him
as we continue on with him in our hearts.
He will always be with us.
For every heartache, every tear, every laugh,
Robert Armstrong will be there.

Dedicated to Robert Armstrong

Norma

Grandma is a loved lady
by more than just family.
Loving her was a great revere,
and we will persevere.
She was full of love.
Now she flies like a dove.
Although she has departed,
she is still lighthearted.
She has left this world.
She was missing her family,
and now she's worry-free,
seeing their smiling faces,
telling of the joyous places.
She's now an angel flying above
as we go on feeling her love.

Dedicated to Norma Boggio

UNEXPECTED POEMS

Into the Blaze

They start work at any hour,
even to be woken up at night.
Putting on their gear in seconds,
they head steadfast to the fight.
Sounding as they go, their alarms,
speeding and flashing lights, as well,
as they go fearless and anxiously
to what we would call hell,
they all go running in
while others are running out.
Their hearts beat and feet pound.
Looking for others they shout.
They are there to rescue us
and always determined to keep us safe,
doing everything they can to stop the fire.

Dedicated to all firefighters

Studying

Studying here, studying there—
all I do is study everywhere.
Studying left, studying right,
studying all day and into the night,
I study and study till my brain is numb,
thinking I will die of boredom.
Instead I fall fast asleep,
in my dreams where I keep
studying here, studying there,
so I am studying everywhere.

The Party Store

Come in and have a blast.
Welcoming you with a smile,
we'll get what you need fast,
taking you to the specific aisle.
If you're not sure what to get,
we will give great party advice,
so your party they won't forget.
We even have party dice,
or maybe you're looking for a hat,
something that looks like Davy Jones.
We have a few that do just that.
Need something for a costume party?
Want to be Sherlock Holmes
or to look like Professor Moriarty?
Planning a loved one's birthday?
We have everything you need.
Already have plates? That's okay.
We have balloons for you indeed,
pretty much everything under the sun.
You'll enjoy coming into the store.
The customer and worker will have fun,
because it's Party America and more.

Dedicated to Billings Party America

My True Love

Your smell wakes me in the early hours.
You lift my spirits when I'm down,
putting a smile on my face before I'm even awake.
The joy you bring is inspirational to all.
I love the way you make me feel,
all warm and fuzzy without a word.
You brighten everyone's face when you enter a room,
knowing you could be with any one of them,
but just for now you are mine, in my hand,
and you will be until you leave me.
When the very last drop touches my tongue,
I shall miss you so, my dearest love,
because nothing hurts more than an empty coffee cup.

Hot Chocolate

Nice and warm on a cold winter day,
tasting all the different flavors—
peanut butter and milk chocolate,
maybe a seasonal gingerbread hot cocoa
and many other interesting ones.
Great for starting a slow morning
or maybe even to brighten an afternoon,
having them topped with whipped cream.
As you drink you feel it warm you up.
The flavors wake up your taste buds,
and the entire day seems brighter.

Chocolate

Chocolate is sweet and tasty,
the melting in your mouth,
smooth and creamy,
the comforting taste of milk chocolate.
I close my eyes and daydream,
the sweet taste of chocolate,
relaxing after a long hard day.

Sleep

Oh, to get a good night's sleep,
without hearing so much as a peep,
to finally be pulled into the abyss
would be like such great bliss.
Feeling so much peace lying in my bed,
having not a single thought run through my head,
slipping away into a perfect fantasy,
all the while feeling completely happy,
but sleep will never come,
leaving me feeling absolutely numb,
wanting sleep more than my strongest desire,
wide awake, as if I were a vampire,
so I say good night and close my eyes,
even though it's all been lies,
for I know when I greet the twilight
I will be restless until the morning light.

Making the Soul Dance

Hearing the music that touches you to your soul,
waking every nerve in your body, you want to lose control,
no matter what you are doing it's relaxing.
It's good to have after a day that's been taxing.

Sitting, standing, or working out you lose yourself in it.
Seeing the change in the people around you, calmness emits.
You start dancing, not giving a care to how you appear,
feeling the music go through you giving you great cheer.

You find with every beat you're tapping your toe,
filling you with joy no matter what the tempo,
listening to your choice of music for hours on end,
it helps your upset or sour mood to mend.

Morning Run

The pounding of your feet
as you run along the street
filling your lungs with air,
wind blowing in your hair,
your heart beating fast,
having energy at long last,
the air so crisp and clear,
with the end drawing near,
you feel exhilarated,
no longer feeling deflated.
It starts to motivate you,
starting your day new.

About the Author

Briana Boggio is a published writer who has been serving in the air national guard for fourteen years and is currently working as a temp tech refueling C-130s. In her spare time, Briana enjoys painting and drawing. This is her first book of poems. She currently lives in Great Falls, Montana.